insight text guide

Sue Sciortino

Selected Poems

Sylvia Plath

First published in 2005, reprinted in 2019, 2023.

Insight Publications Pty Ltd
3/350 Charman Road
Cheltenham VIC 3192
Australia
Tel: +61 3 8571 4950
Fax: +61 3 8571 0257
Email: books@insightpublications.com.au

www.insightpublications.com.au

Sylvia Plath's Selected Poems / Sue Sciortino

A catalogue record for this book is available from the National Library of Australia

ISBNs:
9781921088025 (print)
9781922378583 (digital)
9781922378590 (bundle: print + digital)

Cover design by Gisela Beer, based on a concept by The Modern Art Production Group

Printed by Markono Print Media Pte Ltd

contents

NARRATIVE VOICES & THEMES

narrative voice	effect	key poems
First-person	Intimately engages the reader; used in many poems	'Face Lift' 'Tulips'
Third-person (observer)	Produces a sense of distance from the subject of the poem; used only in a few poems	'Spinster' 'Edge'

themes	images and relationships	key poems
Seeking one's place in the universe; the moon as poetic muse	The moon and nature	'The Moon and the Yew Tree' 'Elm'
Personal growth and rebirth	Hospitalisation (as setting and source of imagery)	'Face Lift' 'Tulips' 'The Stones
	Father figures	'Full Fathom Five' 'Little Fugue' 'Daddy'
The search for a sense of identity	Images of mirrors, reflections, stones, hooks	'Ariel' 'Mirror'
Competing roles of women	Daughter (characterised by feelings of betrayal and inability to communicate)	'Full Fathom Five' 'Daddy'
	Wife (conflicting roles and desires)	'Daddy' 'Tulips' 'Lesbos'
	Mother (many different emotions are depicted)	'Lesbos' 'The Manor Garden' 'Morning Song' 'Nick and the Candlestick'
	Artist (images of sterility, disconnection and/or death)	'Words' 'The Munich Mannequins' 'Edge'

INTRODUCTION

Sylvia Plath's poetry has had a far-reaching influence on both readers and writers since her premature death in 1963. It is valuable for its stylistic accomplishments, as it brings together traditional poetic forms with experimental free-form structures, and for its ability to reach contemporary readers. Her concern with problems such as gender conflicts, sexual inequality and discrimination against women is expressed frankly, particularly in the remarkable poems written shortly before her death.

Although Plath's personal experiences of marriage and of being a female artist in a world dominated by men made her feel both betrayed and powerless, the poetry is not about herself. Rather, it expresses universal values and concerns on behalf of her fellow human beings. The anger and pain that comes through in her work is for the benefit of those of us who suffer dispossession, or battle against established mores that leave us feeling both impotent and vulnerable. We must not, however, mistake her outspokenness on issues that affect women as a platform for feminist ideals. Plath predates the women's revolution of the late 1960s and 1970s, and her concerns are much more inclusive than such a limited application would suggest.

It is also noteworthy that Plath's personal and psychological history is not of primary importance when it comes to analysing her poetry. A concentration on her life circumstances can draw the attention of readers and students away from the poetry, grafting meanings onto the poems that they do not have. Plath manipulated her emotional experiences to make them relevant to larger human issues; otherwise, her poems would not have engaged her readers. The publication of her journals has made it possible for us to know and understand Plath's personal journey, but these must be recognised as a discrete work to be assessed separately from the poetry.

Plath's posthumous award of the Pulitzer Prize for Poetry for *The Collected Poems* recognised her contribution to literature. Beset by mental and physical illness and periods of clinical depression, Plath wrested her art from great darkness. That all Plath's work still remains in print is a testament to her achievement, as is the huge body of critical response her writings have generated. Nevertheless, part of Plath's attraction is that despite our ability to know much about her, she remains as enigmatic to us now as she was to her readers half a century ago.

BACKGROUND & CONTEXT

Sylvia Plath (1932–1963)

The daughter of middle-class immigrants, Sylvia Plath was born in Jamaica Plain, Massachusetts, the older of the two children of Otto and Aurelia Plath. Her father was a professor of German and Entomology (the study of insects) at Boston University; her mother, a high-school teacher, had been his assistant. Both parents valued learning. In 1940, when Sylvia was eight, Otto died of complications after a leg amputation, and Aurelia returned to teaching. Otto's death had far-reaching ramifications for Sylvia, who believed he had betrayed and deserted her. The genetic disposition towards depression that was widespread in Otto's family haunted Sylvia, who was never free of the mental instability that led to her early death.

Due to her mother's influence, Sylvia tried to live up to an old-fashioned feminine ideal of perfection. She attempted to play the role of flawless femininity, becoming a wife and mother with an impeccable record for cooking and domesticity. Her mother's influence was detrimental for Sylvia in many ways because she was always trying to live up to a false, middle-class view when, in fact, the reality of her life warred with her mother's ideal. In *Letters Home* the relationship between mother and daughter is documented, but it is a false document; in reality, there was a distance and lack of comprehension between the two women.[1] Indeed, part of Plath's pain stemmed from her awareness that she was unable to have an honest relationship with her mother, and she struggled against her awareness of that dishonesty.

Although Plath was a brilliant student and seemed supremely confident, she was extremely insecure; she had the highest expectations for herself in her writing, but fulfilled them only at the very end of her life. She tried to balance her domestic role with that of writer, experiencing

[1] Plath, AS (ed.) 1975, *Letters Home: Correspondence 1950–1963*, Harper & Row, New York.

a constant self-doubt that led to depression. She craved recognition, pushing herself relentlessly, and much of her poetry reveals her struggle against both herself and the external world.

It was evident early that writing was to be Plath's vocation. By the time she went to college in the early 1950s she had published poems in newspapers and written over fifty short stories, some of which won prizes. At college she was interested in painting and became quite accomplished in that art, which might explain the predominance of painterly images in her poetry.

In 1953 she suffered a nervous breakdown while attending the prestigious Smith College, Boston. She was given electroconvulsive shock treatments, but in August she attempted suicide. After six months of intensive therapy[2] Sylvia returned to Smith and to her accustomed academic success, but she never fully recovered from her breakdown and her sanity was forever damaged by the shock treatment. For her honours thesis at Smith she wrote on the Russian novelist Dostoyevsky and won a Fulbright Fellowship to study at Cambridge. The title of the thesis, 'The magic mirror: a study of the double in two of Dostoyevsky's novels', is revealing of Plath's later fascination with imagery of the double that is evident through her poetry.

In 1955, she went to England. There she decided to meet the poet Ted Hughes (later to become the Poet Laureate), because his work had impressed her. At Cambridge she felt impelled to combine intensive study with sexual experience, prompted by a rebellion against her mother who could never accept her daughter's sexual involvements. As her writing shows, she protested against double standards in male/female relationships and believed that women could successfully combine sexual passion with intellectual pursuits, as men did.

She and Hughes were married in 1956, with Plath assuming they would have an ideal life together. After she passed her examinations at Cambridge, the Hugheses returned to America where Sylvia taught at

[2] Plath was treated at McLean, the same psychiatric hospital at which the poets Robert Lowell and Anne Sexton were also treated for mental illness.

Smith while investing a great deal of energy into making Ted a success. His first book of poetry, *The Hawk in the Rain*, won a major prize, but Plath found it difficult to develop her own voice as a writer. It was in Boston, too, that Plath worked part-time as a secretary in the psychiatric division of Massachusetts General Hospital, transcribing patients' histories. She was later to use this experience extensively in her poems. She also resumed therapy for her depression.

By 1959 both Plath and Hughes decided that they needed to work professionally on their writing and bravely abandoned their teaching jobs to return to England. Before they left they spent some months at the artists' colony at Yaddo in New York State where Plath produced the first of her most notable poems, 'Poem for a Birthday', where her theme is her own breakdown and suicide attempt in 1953.

In England, Frieda was born and Plath wrote her novel, *The Bell Jar*; her first book of poetry, *The Colossus and Other Poems*, was published in October 1960. It was well received and was subsequently published in the United States. Hughes was becoming well known and was in contact with important poets such as TS Eliot, but the couple had little money. By 1961 these financial difficulties, combined with Plath's jealousy of Hughes' female acquaintances, her self-centredness and the return of her depression, put enormous strains on the marriage.

There were many outbursts of jealous rage. In one incident, Plath became jealous of a female voice on the telephone asking for Hughes. He returned home to find that his work in progress, his notebooks and his precious copy of Shakespeare had all been torn to shreds. The commitment to art that was the mainstay of their marriage crumbled under such assaults. A few days later, in February 1961, Plath miscarried and faced hospitalisation for an appendectomy. It was at this time that she wrote the tender poem 'Morning Song'. While in hospital she was inspired to write 'Tulips', a poem that shows how well she had become the mistress of her imagery, using the colours white and red to convey her imagined death and resurrection. Indeed, after the operation Plath showed a quick return to health, as the hospital had provided a welcome respite from looking after baby Frieda. She returned to writing *The Bell*

Jar but further bouts of depression were not far away. In addition, Plath became pregnant again and started to suffer from isolation and sinus problems.

After the birth of Nicholas in January 1962, Plath faced up to Hughes' infidelity and, as a consequence, began expressing herself through increasingly angry but powerful poems. Hughes and Plath separated. Alone with the children in Devon, Plath wrote most of the poems that later appeared in *Ariel*. After moving to London, in less than two months she produced the forty poems of rage, despair, love and vengeance that made her famous posthumously. These included 'Daddy', 'Poppies in July', 'Ariel', 'The Bee Meeting', and the moving poem to her baby son, 'Nick and the Candlestick'. However, none of the magazines to which she sent these poems accepted them, increasing her depression.

These mature poems reveal a preoccupation with death and rebirth and a recurring theme of the redemption of a meaningless life through art. Fuelled by her anger, her voice became much stronger. Within the framework of her own psychodrama she revealed her tragically wounded personality; her last poems show the point of nihilism, or feelings of nothingness, that she had reached, from which she felt there was no escape except through death. In January 1963, after the publication of *The Bell Jar*, she was engulfed by a deep, clinical depression and on the morning of 11 February she committed suicide. She was just thirty years old.

Plath's poems show that she wrote out of the experience of deep personal pain, and yet she believed in the possibility of a better future for humankind. Although she never fulfilled her own life's promise, she wrote in ways that touch people across cultures and across generations. This is the lasting legacy of her work.

Plath's father

Otto Emil Plath was a German-speaking emigrant from Grabow, a biologist specialising in entomology and the author of *Bumblebees and*

Their Ways (1934). He heavily influenced Sylvia's behaviour, dying when she was eight. She never forgave him for deserting her. The betrayal of the father figure is prominent in many of her poems.

From this figure issues both the historical poems, containing German or Nazi references, and such non-historical work as the bee sequence, where the grief informing the earlier bee poems and the desire to reunite with the dead father are transformed to fury – the same fury revealed in 'Daddy'.

Historical context

Plath's sense of entrapment, her sense that her choices were profoundly limited, is directly connected to the particular time and place in which she wrote poetry. Feminist Betty Friedan describes the late fifties and early sixties for American women as a 'comfortable concentration camp' – physically luxurious, mentally oppressive and impoverished. The recurring metaphors of fragmentation and rebirth, particularly in Plath's late poetry, are, therefore, socially and historically based. She grew up during World War II and this, combined with the politically 'tranquillised fifties' (as Robert Lowell put it), also left a mark on Plath. The images of Nazi concentration camps, cannons, trains, 'wars, wars, wars' (p.52, 'Daddy') and 'Out of a gap/A million soldiers run' (p.58, 'Cut') reflect back to the war, while images of kitchens, refrigerators, adding machines, typewriters and the depersonalisation of hospitals are representations of modern American life in the 1950s.

It is evident from the poems that Plath is very much a woman of the 1950s – educated, intelligent but still restricted in terms of what it was possible for a woman to aspire to. The world she describes in 'The Munich Mannequins' (pp.74–5), for example, is created by men rather than women, since men control the forces of production and their desire to change and dominate the world has transformed women into mere puppets. She sees her era as one of underlying depersonalisation in an economic and social structure that equates people with objects.

Plath was doubly alienated from such a world, objectified by it and, as a female artist, isolated within it. Isolated both from a past tradition and a present community, she found it difficult to structure new alternatives for her own future.

Literary influences

Ted Hughes

Sylvia Plath and Ted Hughes inspired each other to explore new pathways for their respective talents. Their backgrounds were entirely different: he was English and part of the English tradition of writing, while she was American and influenced by the new literary writings in America. Hughes has said that they 'dreamed a lot of shared or complementary dreams'[3] although their methods of writing were entirely different. Plath's was:

> to collect a heap of vivid objects and good words and make a pattern; the pattern would be projected from somewhere deep inside, from her very distinctly evolved myth … Her method was more painterly …[4]

Hughes encouraged her when she was seeking inspiration, and she always sought his approval of her writing. At times, his support enabled her to break out of periods of writer's block. She envied Hughes' ability to work 'unencumbered by any fake image of what the world expects of him'.[5] Nevertheless, she was tireless in promoting Hughes' work, typing and retyping all his manuscripts and taking responsibility for forwarding them to publishers.

Plath's idealisation of Hughes – 'Ted is the ideal, the one possible person'[6] – made his infidelity harder to bear. Paradoxically, though, it

---

3 Interview with Ted Hughes published in the *Paris Review*, Spring 1995, a relevant selection from which is available at http://www.sylviaplath.de/plath/thint.html.

4 Interview with Ted Hughes, http://www.sylviaplath.de/plath/thint.html.

5 Entry for 15 November 1959 in Hughes, T & McCullough, F (eds.) 1991, *The Journals of Sylvia Plath*, Ballantyne Books, New York, p.330.

6 13 October 1959, *Journals*, p.321.

was his betrayal of her that provided the inspiration for the great poems. Writing out of anger and despair, she produced the poems that she is best remembered for: without Hughes, she finally found the independence from him in her writing that she had been seeking.

Robert Lowell

While teaching at Smith College, Boston, Plath attended Robert Lowell's class in poetry writing where she met George Starbuck and Anne Sexton (see below). Lowell remained the poet she admired above all others.[7] He described Plath as 'a brilliant tense presence embarrassed by restraint'.[8] As noted by the poet Dido Merwin, Lowell 'had more than a little in common with Sylvia':[9] both were explosive personalities totally involved in their writing. Some critics have noted Lowell's influence on Plath's own poetics.

Theodore Roethke

While spending the autumn of 1959 at Yaddo writers' colony, Plath discovered Theodore Roethke's poetry, and his work became a decisive influence on her. Both poets had an uneasy German background, and both suffered mental illness from time to time. The poems that make up the sequence 'Poem for a Birthday' are clearly influenced by Roethke's 'mad sequences' but her work is not imitative. Both poets lost their fathers early in life but, while Roethke represented the father figure as fierce and terrifying, Plath represented her father as having betrayed her.

Anne Sexton

Plath and Sexton met in Robert Lowell's writing seminar at Boston University in 1959. Both had attempted suicide and this created a bond between them. Each was aware of the other's poetic output and each constructively criticised the other's work. Some critics have seen

---

7 *Letters Home*, p.407.

8 Stevenson, A 1989, *Bitter Fame: A Life of Sylvia Plath*, Houghton Mifflin, Boston, p.176.

9 *Bitter Fame*, p.336.

resemblances in style between the two poets, dubbing them 'confessional poets'. It is clear, though, that Plath's work is not confessional as such; rather, she uses her personal experiences to develop wider universal themes.

Anne Sexton also committed suicide, but left us with a poem to Sylvia Plath that speaks only of hope for the better world both of them perceived to be possible:

> And I say only
> with arms stretched out into that stone place,
>
> what is your death,
> but an old belonging,
>
> a mole that fell out
> of one of your poems?[10]

Expressionism

Expressionism was a German painters' movement before World War I, characterised by distortion, fragmentation and the communication of violent or stressful emotion. First apparent in the paintings of the Norwegian Edvard Munch, it was a style utilised by such notable painters as Klee, Kandinsky and Modigliani, and came to influence literature, drama, dance, film and music (notably the composer Schoenberg). It was a way of discovering a personal freedom in art whereby the artist expresses only what he or she has within, not what is seen with one's eyes. In other words, it is a style of art in which the intention is not to reproduce a subject accurately, but to portray it in such a way as to express the inner state of the artist. It flowered again during and after World War II as a way of challenging accepted styles in literature and art.

Plath was a widely read and highly educated woman who, with her German background, would have known of and understood the Expressionist movement. In her poems, its influence can be seen in works such as 'Poem for a Birthday' and the later *Ariel* poems.

---

[10] Sexton, A 1963, 'Sylvia's Death', *All Poetry*, https://allpoetry.com/Sylvia's-Death

Surrealism was an offshoot of the Expressionist movement. In poetry, surrealism was the search for a creativity not to be found in the everyday world. It was the expression of a process of thought, free from any control by reason. Many of Plath's poems contain images that could be described as surreal, or more than real and, thus, abstract.

Plath's writings

In addition to her poetry, Plath also wrote many prose works which, unlike the poems, were published throughout her lifetime, culminating in the novel *The Bell Jar*. Even when quite young, she won prizes for her stories and had many of them published. In 1962 she also wrote a verse play for radio, entitled *Three Women*.

In a 1962 radio broadcast, Plath described the difference between writing poetry and prose as one of time. The novelist can gather details over a period and can choose the time she takes. For the poet, on the other hand, time is limited and the poem momentary:

> A door opens, a door shuts. In between you have had a glimpse: a garden, a person, a rainstorm, a dragonfly, a heart, a city … And there is really so little room! So little time! The poet becomes an expert packer of suitcases:
>
> *The apparition of these faces in the crowd;*
> *Petals on a wet black bough.*
>
> There it is: the beginning and the end in one breath. How would the novelist manage that?[11]

It is important that Plath's poems be read in a chronological line of development, more or less as one long poem or a sequence of poems that culminates in the last great poems. She crafted each poem carefully, always conscious of a clear sense of structure where rhyme, stanza, line length and imagery are all designed towards creating a consistent whole.

[11] Plath, S 1977, 'A comparison', broadcast July 1962, reprinted in *Johnny Panic and the Bible of Dreams*, Faber & Faber, London, pp.62–5.

Plath eschewed the contemporary fashion for 'spontaneous' writing and false spontaneity:

> I *cannot* sympathise with these cries from the heart that are informed by nothing except, you know, a needle or a knife, or whatever it is. I believe one should be able to control and manipulate experiences, even the most terrifying, like madness, like being tortured.[12]

Plath came to realise that, unlike prose, poetry gave her the opportunity to focus certain kinds of experience sharply. As her poetic technique matured, she was able to interweave a range of meanings so that the reader is informed of a different set of associations with each subsequent reading. She had the ability to take her readers beyond the merely pictorial and into a state of mind, so that a landscape description, for example, carries another set of signs. She made her poems into psychological explorations through a complex layer of meanings, which the reader is able to experience on several levels simultaneously.

A note on the text

Ted Hughes omitted some of the most important of Sylvia Plath's poems when he chose the *Selected Poems*. Because of this, the following commentary also omits notable poems such as 'Medusa', 'The Arrival of the Bee Box', 'Lady Lazarus', 'Contusion', 'The Applicant', 'Electra on Azalea Path', 'Balloons' and others. These can all be found in *The Collected Poems* (1981).

---

[12] Plath, S 1962, *The Poet Speaks*, Argo Record Co., No. RG455 Lm.

STUDYING POETRY: TECHNIQUES & VOCABULARY

Guidelines for early readings of a poem

1. The first reading of a poem will leave a certain impression, if not a real understanding.
2. Read the poem again – aloud.
   - This is one way of establishing the rhythm of the verses.
   - Notice whether the vocabulary makes you speed up or slow down.
3. Look at the way the poem appears on the page.
   - This will help you establish the form of the poem by noting how regular the lines are.
   - You can see whether the poet uses rhyme as a device by noting how each line ends.
   - Notice the rhyme scheme – the pattern of rhyming words. Do the first two lines rhyme or are the rhyme endings alternate?
   - Are the lines of uneven length without rhyme?
   - Are the verses of uneven length?
   - If so, is there a rhythm built into the verse structure?
   - Are there repeated lines that make a kind of chorus?
   - What does this structure contribute to how readers understand the meaning?
4. Write the poem out line by line with a large space between lines.
   - Examine each word for meaning.
   - Use a dictionary to look up every word.
   - Even if you think you know what a word means it can have other nuances that make an understanding of the poem clearer, or change your initial understanding of the meaning.
   - Write all the meanings under each word.

5 Select significant images like colours, animals, trees, moon, sun, mirrors and hooks.
   - Images are used by poets to enhance the meaning of what they are trying to convey.
   - Some poets use their knowledge of myth and legend to enrich their images.
   - The symbols are used to make the ordinary memorable and the simple complex.

6 Write out in prose your new understanding of the poem using the dictionary meanings.

7 Read the poem again and discuss it with someone else.
   - Does your interpretation coincide with the other person's?
   - If not, try to convince the other person.
   - Does the other person contribute something new to your understanding?

You should now be able to write a paragraph on what you think the poet is trying to express.

Write another paragraph on how the structure contributes to your understanding of the poem, and how the poet has used devices and images to communicate meaning.

Poetic diction: definitions and examples of common poetic devices

Poetry differs from everyday speech and prose fiction in that its language is usually more intense and figurative. The term 'poetic diction' refers to a poet's (or any writer's) special language, and covers the words, phrases and poetic devices that are not used in ordinary speech or are used in special ways. At various periods in literature, poets have used 'elevated' language to convey the beauty and nobility of their thoughts. At other times, especially in the twentieth century, poets have experimented with new approaches to capture the immediacy of lived experience, and so poetic language has become much more varied. Sylvia Plath's poetry depicts her quest for poetic inspiration and vision, which gradually turns from a search in the external world to a search directed inward, towards the self, seeking enlightenment through self-examination. Finally, her last poems show her seeking the perfection of the self, which seems attainable only through death.

In order to analyse poetic diction, you need to know and understand the most common poetic devices that are used. These are listed with brief definitions below. (For more detailed definitions, see a reputable dictionary of literary terms.)

1 Establish the *persona* – the person speaking in the poem (see the notes under 'Narrative voices' as well). The word *persona* comes from the Latin word for 'mask' and was originally applied to drama. In poetry, the persona is often the first-person narrator of a poem.

2 How does the *form* the poet has used contribute to readers' understanding of what the poem is about? Why do different poets adopt different verse forms? Plath's poems vary in form, from free verse to lyrics to highly patterned stanzas:

   - six free verse three-line stanzas in 'Morning Song' (p.23)
   - two unrhyming nine-line stanzas in 'Mirror' (p.34)
   - four regular, though unusual, nine-line stanzas in 'Finisterre' (pp.31–2)
   - fourteen irregular three-line verses in 'Elm' (pp.43–4)
   - seven irregular unrhyming two-line couplets followed by a single line in 'Poppies in July' (p.45).

3 Does the *rhythm* (metre) evoke an emotional response?

4 How does the *rhyme* scheme help to make the poem effective?

   - Line rhyme supports meaning in many of Plath's poems, as does internal rhyme and a combination of both:
     'Homunculus, I am ill./I have taken a pill to kill' (p.58).
   - Most of her poems are in free verse, therefore lacking a rhyme pattern.

- It is interesting to examine her other ways of creating sound patterns, such as in 'Maudlin' (p.6), which uses a hard 'g' at the end of the first and fourth lines in both stanzas as a kind of rhyming pattern – 'hag', 'egg', 'swig' and 'leg'.

5 How does abandoning formal metre and rhyme – free verse – contribute to a poem's effectiveness?

- 'Resolve' (p.7) abandons any attempt at formal verse patterns.

6 What kind of *vocabulary* is used?

- Is the poem packed with adjectives and adverbs?
- Is it purely descriptive?
- How are contrasting words used for effect?

7 What kind of *emotional response* does the language elicit?

- Does it make the reader feel sad, happy, angry or some other emotion?
- Is the reader's sympathy engaged?
- Is this the response the poet intends?

8 What kind of *tone* does the poet use? The tone suggests the attitude of the speaker or persona towards their listener and subject matter. To identify the tone (which can change within a poem), read the poem aloud.

- Is the tone solemn, angry, serious, ironic, bitter?
- Is there a reliance on devices such as sarcasm, wit and persuasion to win over readers?

9 Is the *voice* used in the poem private or public? Is it one of a

- storyteller
- commentator
- reporter
- reflection
- bystander
- observer?

10 What *devices* does the poet employ to manipulate the reader's response?

- *Similes* – comparisons beginning with 'as' or 'like'. Plath uses similes extensively to create the effects she seeks:
  - '*like* a fat gold watch' (p.23)
  - 'clear vowels rise *like* balloons' (p.23)
  - '*like* a terrible fish' (p.34)
  - 'pears fatten *like* little buddhas' (p.15).
- *Metaphors* – comparisons in which one thing is described as another:
  - 'Little poppies, little hell flames' (p.45)
  - 'in its strangle of branches' (p.44)
  - 'Tongue a rose-colored arrow' (p.13)
  - 'Little bloody skirts!' (p.45).
- *Alliteration* – repetition of consonants for emphasis:
  - 'Palely and flamily' (p.64)
  - 'Mud-mattressed' (p.6)
  - 'surface seldom' (p.9)
  - 'Full fathom five' (p.9).
- *Personification* – giving an inanimate object human attributes:
  - 'I am silver and exact' (a mirror, p.34)
  - 'the last fingers, knuckled and rheumatic,/Cramped on nothing' (an outcrop of land, p.31)
  - 'I have suffered the atrocity of sunsets' (an elm tree, p.43).
- *Assonance* – repetition of vowel sounds:
  - 'S**ou**ls, r**o**lled in the doom-noise of the sea' (p.31)
  - 'p**i**nk f**i**zz' (p.58).
- *Onomatopoeia* – imitating sounds of objects:
  - 'crackle and drag' (p.77)
  - 'The potatoes hiss' (p.55).

11 What kinds of *images* promote an understanding of what the poet is trying to convey?

12 What makes the poem *memorable*?

PLATH'S USE OF IMAGERY

One way of approaching a response to Plath's poetry is through the imagery she uses to dramatise human life, often using her own emotional state to extend or examine the range of human experiences. Plath's poems are dark and moody in their imagery and frequently use starkly contrasting images to highlight the main thought she is conveying. Imagery is often used as a structural device, as well as to focus the emotions of readers.

As an explanation of the sources of her own poetic technique and her use of imagery, Plath noted that, for example, she was concerned with the issues of nuclear warfare and with the relationship, in America in particular, between big business and the military. She did not, however, choose to write overtly about these issues, but they influenced her 'in a sidelong fashion':

> My poems do not turn out to be about Hiroshima, but about a child forming itself finger by finger in the dark. They are not about the terrors of mass extinction, but about the bleakness of the moon over a yew tree in a neighbouring graveyard. Not about the testaments of tortured Algerians, but about the night thoughts of a tired surgeon.[13]

This is an indication of the complex way Plath's imagery works. A poem's meaning exists on several levels at the same time and is achieved through a layering effect of images and ambiguity to extend its range. To achieve her desired effects, Plath relies heavily on metaphor and simile, colour and allusion. It is through these that we must unpack, as it were, the layers of meaning to get to the central idea of each poem.

[13] Plath, S, 'Context', reprinted in *Johnny Panic*, pp.98–9.

The moon and the natural world

The moon is a central symbol in Plath's poetry. She makes over a hundred direct references to it in this volume. Usually, it operates as her poetic muse, symbolising the source and inspiration for her poetic vision. It operates as a symbol of her vocation as a poet and often stands for her female biology. The natural world is characterised in Plath's poems by process, by the ebb and flow of months and seasons, by a continual dying and rebirth. The moon, then, is a symbol for the monthly ebb and flow of the tides and of the cycles in a woman's body. This contrasts with Plath's use of symbols for the social world, the world of the city, which is defined as male and is separated from the natural world. Winter in the city, for example, is grim; it suggests death rather than hibernation, and cold often represents perfection or sterility. In the countryside, though, winter is presented as a time of rest or the renewal of the seasonal cycle that is equated with rebirth.

Plath, however, must not be mistaken for a 'nature' poet. Often she demonstrates, through her personas, that she is not really at home in the countryside, but she uses the moods of landscapes or weather metaphorically for her thoughts and emotions. She does not express any genuine pleasure in nature as such, and in the last poems, settings become more and more metaphoric to represent a human protagonist's inner thoughts and emotions.

Symbolism of the yew tree

Extending the metaphor of the moon, in 'The Moon and the Yew Tree' (p.33) the yew tree becomes a powerful image that seems to interact with the moon. Clearly Plath has two referents here – Christian symbols and nature. Neither, however, seems to offer redemption; there is only 'blackness and silence' (p.33).

Key point

Although Ted Hughes explains this poem as being Plath's rendering of her mother mourning in heaven and her father lying under the roots of the yew tree, this seems to be a simplistic reading that does not allow for the poem's true range of meaning, nor does it explain the variety of images that Plath employs.

Although it is the central image of the poem, the yew tree itself does not appear until the third stanza. The first two stanzas allude to the way the mind organises thoughts, triggered by the parallel between the mind and what the eye sees, as the opening lines suggest: 'This is the light of the mind, cold and planetary./The trees of the mind are black. The light is blue'. What Plath actually sees from her bedroom window in Devon is the yew tree silhouetted against the moon in a churchyard cemetery on a misty night. But that is not what she is writing about. Rather, she is setting up a painterly picture that extends to the patterning of the thought process. The scene is a metaphor for a state of mind and sets in motion a whole set of associations that equate with the way the imagination processes images and memories. The poem tries to approximate the way in which thoughts move and memories intersect with one another.

The first stanza makes immediate reference to God and the Christian ideal of 'humility', but it is 'the grasses' that metaphorically adopt an attitude of supplication towards the speaker, 'as if' *she* 'were God'. The speaker is processing thoughts that lead through the gloomy images of 'spiritous mists' and 'a row of headstones' to the conclusion that 'I simply cannot see where there is to get to' – in other words, there does not appear to be a path to redemption from the pain and suffering we experience.

The moon is the dominant image of the second stanza. It does not provide a 'door' through which the speaker can reach salvation or relief from human pain. Rather, it is presented as remote and distant, which in reality it is, but the speaker is looking to it to provide a solution to the human predicament. The language here is interesting, for the moon, metaphorically, 'drags the sea after it like a dark crime', but it is also, colloquially, 'terribly upset'. The simplicity of the latter, contrasting with the complexity of the metaphor, is most arresting. At the same time the moon's face reflects 'the O-gape of complete despair', almost a personification of this fixed object, suggesting it is capable of some kind of emotion.

But the speaker's moon-gazing is abruptly interrupted with the interposing of the staccato statement, 'I live here'. We are startled out of our own preoccupation with the moon as our attention is drawn back to the speaker. These three words have the effect both of reminding us that the speaker is the central figure of the poem, that it is about her, and of locating us back within the landscape on earth. The impact of this is to divide the images of the moon from the religious images that follow, and yet both sets of images are concerned with a female figure. The Christian imagery then becomes the focus, as in the first stanza, as the church bells 'startle the sky' and affirm 'the Resurrection'. But even they have a persona because they 'bong out their *names*'. The 'Resurrection', combined with 'God' and 'humility' in the first stanza, heightens the image of the woman seeking some kind of answers to her own 'griefs' and the 'black[ness]' of her thoughts.

It is at this point that the third stanza finally introduces the yew tree, a motif that is not only central to the poem but also almost iconic in its significance. It is here that the images of the tree and the moon take on other connotations, for the tree is clearly a phallic symbol, it 'points up' and is, therefore, male, while the moon is couched in female terms of 'mother' and 'Mary', the mother of God. The yew tree is also 'Gothic' in shape, echoing the neighbouring church spire that reaches up to heaven, while the moon connects heaven with earth. This is a complex interweaving of male and female symbolism with the symbols of Christianity to further the idea that the speaker is supplicating the moon. There is, however, something almost sinister about the maleness of the yew tree, setting up a dichotomy between its masculine dominance and the female 'face in its own right', an assertion of female independence.

Yet, it is apparent that the moon, although female, has failed the speaker for 'She is not sweet like Mary' and, further, she is associated with the negative image of 'small bats and owls'. Her 'blue garments', most likely the sky, remind us of the traditional blue gown of the Holy Mary, who represents relief from pain. The line 'How I would like to believe in tenderness' once more brings the speaker to centre stage, for it is she who seeks 'tenderness', notably not for everyone, but for herself 'in particular' through entreaty to a gentle and 'mild' virginal saint who is starkly compared with the harsh moon. This line expresses the yearning behind all Plath's poetry.

The first line of the last stanza extends the Christian symbolism, for the speaker has 'fallen a long way', implying some kind of a fall from grace for which she needs redemption, although it would be a misreading to see this as a lament for lost salvation. Outside, in a lovely and arresting image, 'Clouds are flowering/Blue and mystical over the face of the stars' in contrast with the inside of the church where the saints float 'over the cold pews,/Their hands and faces stiff with holiness'. The coldness and the stiff faces suggest that Christianity has, after all, no answers for the speaker's personal pain and that she cannot communicate with them. When Plath says, 'the moon is my mother' she is saying that she herself is wild, criminal, despairing and bald. This implies that she has inherited bad ways from her mother.

Finally, 'the message of the yew tree is blackness – blackness and silence'. The symbolic male dominates the scene, proudly manipulating everything around it, leaving the final idea, perhaps, that the moon and the yew tree are antagonists in a drama that excludes us. More significantly, these two images reinforce the recurring struggle between male and female that pervades Plath's work.

We can examine the position of the speaker in regard to the two sets of images if we extract the five instances of the use of the personal pronoun, 'I', and read them as follows:

> The grasses unload their griefs on my feet as if I were God. I simply cannot see where there is to get to. I live here. How I would like to believe in tenderness. I have fallen a long way.

This narrative thread suggests that the speaker is part of the whole universe, like the moon, the stars, the birds and the yew tree, but that she is manipulated by that universe. It also implies that she is unable to find her particular identity within the universe, especially in view of the male dominance that surrounds her.

- The colour 'blue' is mentioned four times in the poem. How do these images relate to one another?
- The line 'I simply cannot see where there is to get to' stands as a metaphor for Plath's search for something significant in her life beyond love and beyond her vocation.

A later and more desperate expression of male/female antagonism can be found in another tree poem, 'Elm' (pp.43–4). It documents the tensions in a marriage – suspicions, hurt, jealousy and anger – and, once more, utilises the image of the moon in relation to a large tree.

Mirror images: 'Mirror'

Key point

Plath often uses images of mirrors and water as poetic devices to reflect her own emotional state.

'Mirror' (p.34) is Plath's most overt expression of a metaphor for the struggle between the true and false selves. The mirror is a device that enables us to examine our inner selves as well as our outer reflected images. The mirror becomes a symbol of female passivity, of subjugation and of Plath's own conflicted self-identity as she tackles the complex issue of human identity.

The opening – 'I am silver and exact' – suggests initially that the mirror can only reflect reality: we cannot find our true selves in a reflection. She personifies the mirror with the use of the first-person pronoun, suggesting that it is an active participant in our lives. Being neutral, it has 'no preconceptions' and is 'unmisted by love or dislike'; it has no emotional connection with what is reflected in it. And yet, the statement

'I am not cruel, only truthful' is not altogether accurate because what we see as our physical reflection in the mirror causes us either joy or pain. We are either satisfied with our physical form or, sometimes, emotionally destroyed by it as we measure ourselves against socially accepted ideals of beauty. The cold and impartial tone suggests that the mirror can, indeed, be 'cruel'. While the mirror does not lie, the mind, however, can deceive and hide the real self behind the physical self and, thus, the mirror is transformed from a passive reflector to an active speaker.

The poet recognises that the mirror is, in fact, 'a little god' able to 'meditate' as the glass both hides and reflects those that look into it. It is worth enjoying the complexity of this image. Read literally, the mirror says that it is constantly being separated from the pink and speckled wallpaper, which it thinks is part of its heart, by people who come between it and the wall, as well as by the repeated fall of night. If the wallpaper is 'its heart' then the mirror has no real heart or emotions. The faces that separate the mirror from its paper heart symbolise the separation of the inner self we seek and our outer, reflected forms.

You can, however, read a different story in the poem. By transposing the mirror and the speaker (which are, after all, images of each other at some level) the poem is an acknowledgment that, symbolically, we seek in the mirror our inner self as well as the reflected form. And so the paradox of the mirror is established: we cannot find the true self there, we can only reflect the outer physical image when what we really seek is self-knowledge.

The 'mirror' changes to a 'lake' in the second stanza. On one reading, we understand that the woman turns to candles and the moon, because unlike a mirror, which is exact, candlelight and moonlight give off a soft, flattering light that makes us look more glamorous than we really are. The woman identifies her real self with her idealised, glamorised image (this is the pathos of femininity: where people identify their inner being with what they look like).

On another level we see the mirror reflecting a woman who is 'Searching my reaches for what she really is'. The woman is shown as passive, depersonalised, victimised and helpless – 'She rewards me with tears and an agitation of hands' – as the lake reflects her coming and going 'faithfully' and now seems to be more emotionally involved with the woman.

The lake/mirror exudes its own sense of importance: 'I am important to her'. Every day the woman comes at dawn – 'Each morning it is her face that replaces the darkness' – in a passive acceptance of her life as it is. But it is not a matter of mere vanity or a desire to stay young that 'In me she has drowned a young girl'. It is, rather, that as she leaves youth behind and matures, she is seeking her real self and is both fascinated and repelled by the glass that simultaneously hides and reflects her true self. The last simile – 'like a terrible fish' – is not so much an image of ageing and decay but more a suggestion that the woman's personal demon is concealed and that, however much she searches for it in her reflection, it does not emerge or 'Rise'. Rather, the monstrous self remains concealed behind her own distorted image. Plath understands that woman are afraid of being physically old and unattractive and, thus, unloveable.

The mirror/lake becomes the enemy that, instead of recording the natural maturation process of a young woman, is reinterpreted as drawing the woman towards the 'terrible fish' of her future self.

The short sentences such as 'I am silver and exact. I have no preconceptions' and 'I am important to her. She comes and goes' slow the tempo and create dramatic pauses that underline the theatricality of the device of the mirror/lake speaker. At the same time, they serve to emphasise the idea that the search for self-knowledge involves the kind of brutal honesty that the mirror represents.

Key point

The mirror is a central image for Plath because it shows that rather than looking outwards to see the real world, one must turn inward to a reflected image for answers.

A mirror/lake cannot provide any response because it is reflecting the self over and over; it cannot reveal the self as part of the wholeness of the universe and, therefore, circles in on itself. To be reborn, Plath suggests, we must overcome the physical world as well as the world of the emotions.

- Unusually, Plath uses two nine-line stanzas here. Each acts as a separate chapter in establishing a central image and advancing the narrative, like a story.
- Look at other examples of the use of the reflected image in the poems. How does its meaning vary?
- The lines 'and in me an old woman/Rises towards her day after day, like a terrible fish' is a poetic conceit that aptly describes the ageing process.

Plath's preoccupation with the mirror as a metaphor for the struggle between the true and false self suggests that courage is required to accept that we cannot hide behind a false representation of the self, but must strive to reconcile outward appearance and inner reality. The mirror is one of the images that links Plath's poems into one complete oeuvre, reinforcing the idea that her poems, at least from 'The Stones' onwards, should be considered as a sequence rather than merely as individual poems.

Images of motherhood: 'The Manor Garden' and 'Morning Song'

Written at Yaddo in 1959 while she was pregnant, 'The Manor Garden' (p.15) shows the direction of Plath's use of nature. Particulars from nature are used to parallel and explain the growth of a foetus in a woman's body. But the prospect of birth is not a joyful one, for the tone of the poem is one of apprehension. The summer has passed and now 'The fountains are dry and the roses over'. As an opening line, this conjures up a negative mood, which is followed by 'Incense of death'. Plath was on the eve of two 'difficult borning[s]' at this time. Not only was she pregnant with her first baby, but she had made the difficult decision to become a full-time, professional writer without the prop of an academic teaching job. From this point, both she and her husband were to depend on their writing to make a living.

Although the tone of foreboding is maintained through the poem, the baby is shown as growing relentlessly towards the moment of birth when she will inherit both the past and what is likely to be an uncertain future, as does Plath as both a mother and a writer. After the sombre opening, the foetus is referred to explicitly with 'Your day approaches'. The analogy of her growth is made with the pleasing simile, 'The pears fatten like little buddhas', showing fruitfulness in the midst of death and a fading summer, but this is a singular image of joy at the prospect of new life.

The second stanza illustrates how the foetus begins to assume a human shape with 'Head, toe and finger' coming 'clear of the shadow'. The images in the third stanza are intricate, hinting at the complexities that this new life will face. Positive images give way to negative ones. The 'fluted columns' of ancient Greek buildings, representing the great artistic achievements of our culture, are broken. The acanthus symbolises growth and immortality, though Christ's crown of thorns was made of acanthine. While white heather is a sign of good luck, the crow has symbolic significance both good and bad. Perhaps the scavenger crow waits to pick over the emotional carcass. Even more telling is the particular family history of 'Two suicides' and the enduring human condition marked by 'Hours of blankness' with 'Some hard stars' that impassively watch over every human life. As these negative images outweigh the positive aspects of a human birth, the prophecy is for 'a difficult borning'.

With the exception of the simile in the first stanza, there is no joy in either the prospect of birth or in the natural world that surrounds the baby. Wolves, spiders, worms and crows suggest an entry into a cold and bleak world that provides no comfort to humans either physically or emotionally. Both the poet and the baby confront a difficult future.

Plath has not yet established the poetic diction that characterises her later poems. For example, the form and rhythm are not of particular note, in contrast to the sharp rhythms and forms she was to adopt in the last poems.

The negativity of birth and motherhood in 'The Manor Garden' is somewhat counteracted by the images in 'Morning Song' (p.23), which is set after the birth of a baby. Here Plath explores the complex interrelationship between a mother and her new baby. There is the realisation that this baby now exists independently of the mother while being utterly dependent on her, that she is strong yet fragile and threatened by all kinds of dangers, including some kind of possible negligence by the mother/speaker.

Key point

The images in 'Morning Song' illustrate the complexity of Plath's poetic diction as she conveys a sense of warmth and life only to undercut it with ideas of transience and mortality.

The mother gets up at dawn to feed her baby. The first line is celebratory, for 'Love' is the first word of the poem, indicating that this was a joyful union that produced the baby. The simile 'like a fat gold watch' suggests both health and a strong heartbeat, the inexorable pulse of life. The slowing down of the rhythm with these three monosyllabic words precisely mirrors the ticking of the clock and, thus, life being measured against the rhythmic march of time. However, the image also indicates something cold and mechanical, suggesting contrary states of mind of the mother. This image could also parallel a moon image, connecting the baby with Plath's recurring moon symbol that represents the poetic muse, suggesting that her own baby's birth has, perhaps, renewed her desire for creativity, a rebirth of her art.

Through the mother's recollection we witness the moment of birth as the midwife 'slap[s]' the 'footsoles' and the baby begins to cry. The 'bald cry' (bawled) expresses the aloneness of this now unprotected life as she takes her place in the world, subject now to the impassive 'elements', to be buffeted by life's experiences. This is reinforced by the absence of any warm feeling of the baby being held in the mother's arms, receiving comfort or affection.

The first two tercets herald the baby's birth, but the image of the plump, precious life ('fat gold watch') is undercut by the 'echo[ing]' voices and the metaphor of the baby as a 'New statue./In a drafty museum', not a comforting image. The parents appear to be helplessly standing around gazing at this new phenomenon, a baby, recognising both its vulnerability and their own. They are overwhelmed, inadequate and somewhat alienated. This suggests that the mother is detached and the 'drafty museum' is the impersonal hospital ward. There do not seem to be any of the usual expressions of delight associated with the birth of a new baby.

The third stanza records the complicated reaction of the mother who has given birth. She is now in her own home but feels separate from the new baby. It is no longer a part of her, but an independent life; the poem creates a tension between her ties with the baby and her recognition of its separateness from her. With her 'Effacement', she feels a sense of loss of her own individuality while she watches over the 'moth-breath' that symbolises self-sufficient life in the breathing baby. The cloud image suggests ephemerality, insubstantiality, while the mirror reflects her own sense of displacement of the self, a sense that the promise of bonding between mother and baby is not automatic. As is usual in Plath, the mirror is an important symbol, and here its reflecting image works as part of the mother's 'Effacement' as the child assumes independence from the mother. Plath is contemplating the transience of the mother–child relationship and uses the conceit of the 'cloud' as a comparison for motherhood.

The picture seems idealised with its images of 'pink roses', floral 'nightgown', 'stars' and 'balloons', but this is, again, undercut by the physical dependence of the child that demands lactation – 'Your mouth opens clean as a cat's' – rather than affection from the mother. There is a sense of duty as the mother 'stumble[s] from bed, cow-heavy', roused from her own sleep to attend to the child's needs as 'The window square/Whitens and swallows its dull stars', a metaphor for dawn that uniquely presents the moment that light overtakes darkness and heralds a new day. With that new day comes also a lighter, more joyous feeling from the mother that the baby's tentative 'handful of notes', the baby's 'Morning Song', enable her to apprehend the child's freedom rising 'like balloons', yet it is a freedom lost to the adult.

With a real honesty, Plath explores the ways in which the speaker experiences the situation of motherhood – her feelings and attitudes, whether explicit or implicit. In so doing, she elicits a shock of recognition from other mothers who all experience this complicated mixture of joy and 'mourning', for the title implies both a celebration and a kind of grief for the severance of a unique interdependence in pregnancy between the unborn child and the mother. There is also the ambivalence of the realisation that with new life comes new responsibilities and a necessary loss of individuality for the mother.

- These three-line stanzas (tercets), act to propel the action forward, setting up an inward rhythm, despite the lack of a traditional rhyme scheme.

Images of sterility

Despite the warmth of her 'baby' poems, Plath did not relish the idea of motherhood, yet as a woman of the fifties she was socially bound to the ideology of the family. As a female writer she was under pressure to conform to the ideal of domesticity as created in the contemporary women's magazines. Consequently, in her poetry there is a definable resentment of men who seemed to have the best of all worlds; she envied their freedom to have both a career and a family life. These feelings become more complex as she grapples with the sense of betrayal that the early death of her father left.

'The Munich Mannequins'

This clash between the creativity of men and women can be seen through both the winter landscape and the images of barrenness that characterise 'The Munich Mannequins' (pp.74–5). Like the other poems that see humanity reduced to near nothingness, this poem was written in the last, most productive phase of Plath's life, just a few days before her death. The first line 'Perfection is terrible, it cannot have children' sets the tone of desolation that is the essence of the poem. For the setting she chooses Munich, a place of unhappy memories of her own visit to Germany in 1956 and connected with her exploration of Nazism evident in other poems, such as 'Daddy' (pp.52–4). In 'The Munich Mannequins' she describes the city as a 'morgue', a cold, empty place between two cities of warmth and colour – 'Paris and Rome'. Perfection in 'The Munich Mannequins' suggests something artificially created and is equated with the deadening of women by the male quest for perfection. The mannequins, presented as 'Orange lollies on silver sticks', represent the visual ideal of perfect women, yet they are the opposite of female roundness, particularly in pregnancy.

These store dummies are sterile, they are 'Naked and bald', stripped of any resemblance to women. Their wombs are empty and 'The tree of life/Unloosing their moons, month after month, to no purpose' means that the menstrual flow is a waste because it brings no life and is symbolic, therefore, of sterility and unfulfilled womanhood. Their childlessness, presented as a kind of perfection, is the opposite of nature because all life is denied.

The yew tree is a symbol of both death and regeneration. The Hydra, a mythical many-headed creature that could regrow its heads if they were cut off, lived in a swamp. Hercules killed it as his second task. Thus the second stanza is a very complex reflection on both real images and classical metaphor. In a literal sense the yew trees the poet observes in Devon are blown around at night, their branches assuming multiple forms. They 'give birth' to the new moon (which rises above the yew tree) twelve times a year. Metaphorically, the symbol of life gives birth to moons that are sterile. Note the moving contrast between wet (blood, the Hydra) and dry (air, the moon).

The mannequins replace actual women and represent the objectification of women by men. The only remaining sign of a woman's presence is 'the domesticity of these windows,/The baby lace, the green-leaved confectionery'. Men, on the other hand, are described in terms of their shoes and their presence in the anonymity of hotel corridors where 'Hands will be opening doors and setting/Down shoes for a polish of carbon/Into which broad toes will go tomorrow'. People, Plath suggests, lose a sense of their wholeness and are dehumanised – 'Nobody's about' – and become recognisable only through their parts: 'shoes', 'Hands', 'lace' curtains. Finally, there is nothing left.

In 'The Munich Mannequins', men, whom Plath sees as responsible for this fragmentation, have gone much further than controlling the means of production; they have transformed woman into a puppet, a mannequin – there is only 'Voicelessness' – which provides the final solution to the problems of female creativity and self-determination.

Key point

As in the other *Ariel* poems, Plath sees the result of women's lives being ultimately a product of male domination as a total depersonalisation of the social world, leading to isolation whereby both men and women suffer.

- The two-line stanzas (couplets) match the bleakness of the language. There are no flowery adjectival descriptions, just language stripped bare to make the greatest impact.
- Look carefully at the images of coldness that set the bleak tone.
- Plath uses recurring images of the colour black, and her symbol of emotional predation, hooks, also appears in this poem.
- What is the effect of the repetition of 'glittering' at the end of the poem?

- Plath employs another image of a yew tree[14] that apparently represents an empty womb. Compare this usage with that in 'The Moon and the Yew Tree', discussed on pages 19–23.

'Edge'

Plath's last poem, 'Edge' (p.77), brings together some of her central images, notably those of motherhood and the moon. While the tone is less overtly one of desperation than in 'The Munich Mannequins', there is, nevertheless, a sense of climax in the composition of the figures arranged for theatrical effect. If we did not know that this was the last poem she wrote there would still be an aesthetic impression of finality about the woman pictured as the central figure. After the first line of 'The Munich Mannequins' – 'Perfection is terrible' – here, 'The woman is perfected': she is, in fact, dead! This suggests that Plath had come to believe, ultimately, that only in death could 'woman' achieve what was not possible in life. The first line of the second couplet would seem to substantiate this view, for the body in death 'wears the smile of accomplishment' that Plath suggests is denied to woman in life.

Unlike so many of Plath's poems that employ a first-person speaker, this poem is narrated in the third person as if to further distance this figure from life. The woman is pictured as a Greek marble statue, suggesting a timeless classicism in 'the scrolls of her toga' and a serenity in giving up the struggle to find an answer to the complex demands on a woman's life. The two 'dead' children have been provided for, having been fed with the 'Pitcher of milk, now empty' and then 'She has folded/Them back into her body' to save them. The woman is 'perfected' because she has reversed her maternal functions and taken the children back into her. The lovely simile 'as petals/Of a rose close' at night aptly describes how the children have been sheltered from further harm.

In this merciless foreshadowing of what was to come in Plath's own life, the poem has an overwhelming power – beautiful, yet grim. The

[14] From Merwin, D, 'Vessel of Wrath: A Memoir of Sylvia Plath', quoted in Stevenson, *Bitter Fame*, p.330.

last two couplets concern the moon, symbolic for Plath of her poetic muse. Personified, the moon watches over this statue-like body, but no longer provides inspiration. The woman has 'come so far, it is over' and the moon, ancient goddess and muse, need not grieve, for this is neither unexpected nor unusual. 'She is used to this sort of thing' as she has seen so many women give up their tussle with their own creativity, with the striving for recognition in a world denoted by male symbols and male language signifiers.

In 'Edge', Plath has finally become the tragic heroine of her own construction. The line 'We have come so far, it is over' provides a fitting epitaph for a writer who died by her own hand at the point of creativity that promised so much more.

- The final image of the personified moon, 'Her blacks crackle and drag', is a remarkable example of onomatopoeia where the sound echoes the sense of the phrase.
- The form of two-line couplets serves to bring the action forward quite rapidly, as it also does in 'The Munich Mannequins'. Why do you think Plath adopted this form for these late poems?

Colour imagery

While the colour red is dominant in Plath's poems, the neutral colours – black and white – feature more consistently. Often red is contrasted with white, setting the symbol for blood against that of purity. Green, on the other hand, is usually used as a background, while blue ranges from the azure of sky to a dark ink blue or a thin blue, the colour of light. As the language becomes sparer and the patterns of imagery are stripped down to single words and phrases, colours are applied like a painter's deft brushstroke to enhance the desired effect.

The following examples show some of the ways Plath uses colour as part of the rich, allusive imagery characteristic of her poetry.

'Ariel'

- 'Nigger-eye/Berries … Black sweet blood mouthfuls' (p.62) – a concrete image symbolising sensuousness.
- 'Into the red/Eye, the cauldron of morning' (p.63) – an image of a fiery sunrise.

'By Candlelight'

- 'A sort of black horsehair' (p.60) – night.
- 'Steeled with the sheen/Of what green stars' (p.60) – night as patterned upholstery.
- 'a dull blue dud' (p.60) – candle burning low.
- 'The yellow knife/Grows tall' (p.60) – fully lit candle.
- 'Hefting his white pillar with the light' (p.61) – the candle.
- 'The sack of black!' (p.61) – a further image of night.

'Insomniac'

- 'The night sky is only a sort of carbon paper,/Blueblack' (p.27) – night.
- 'A bonewhite light' (p.27) – intrusive starlight.
- 'He is immune to pills: red, purple, blue' and 'Their poppy-sleepy colors' (p.27) – medication for insomnia.
- 'His head is a little interior of gray mirrors' (p.27) – the mind projecting and reflecting images that prevent the subject from sleeping.
- 'his white disease' (p.28) – insomnia.
- 'eyes mica-silver and blank' (p.28) – the early morning bleary eyes of workers.

Other important patterns of imagery

Images of effacement are common, such as people represented by the thinness of paper:

- 'Black lake, black boat, two black, cut-paper people' (p.41, 'Crossing the Water')
- 'The thin/Papery feeling' (p.59, 'Cut')
- 'a cut-paper shadow' (p.25, 'Tulips').

Images of hooks have negative connotations often used to tie the poem's persona to life:

- 'Nigger-eye/Berries cast dark/Hooks' (p.62, 'Ariel')
- 'Looking, with its hooks, for something to love' (p.44, 'Elm')
- 'To trade their hooks for hands' (p.17, 'The Stones').

NARRATIVE VOICES

Personas or speakers

Most of these poems tell a story through a speaker or narrator that, in poetry, is called a 'persona'. It is important to work out the poem's story, mini-drama, or central thought or feeling before beginning an analysis of its features. By establishing who the narrator/persona is, it is then possible to gauge what kind of voice and tone the poet is using.

Often Plath's personas are first-person singular, 'I', speakers who recount their experiences directly to readers. This enables Plath to engage her readers more intimately and to involve them personally in the experience.

First-person narrative voice in 'Face Lift'

Many of the characters in these poems reflect Plath's own inner conflicts, but the speaker and the poet are not necessarily one and the same. In 'Face Lift' (pp.21–2), for example, she is recounting the experiences of plastic surgery in great detail in the first person, but this is not her own experience. Rather, it was the experience of an acquaintance, Dido Merwin:

> When Sylvia asked questions and expressed interest in my incisions and spectacular technicolour bruises it seemed perfectly natural ... The scooping of my face lift was a unique interlude in our rather ambivalent relationship.[15]

Plath, as a poet, merely uses this account as material for her interest in the possibility or, perhaps, the necessity of rebirth.

---

[15] From Merwin, D, 'Vessel of Wrath: A Memoir of Sylvia Plath', quoted in Stevenson, *Bitter Fame*, p.330.

Her first-person singular narrator experiences the wonder of regeneration through plastic surgery in an ironic discourse on a woman's seemingly miraculous casting off of old age. This first stanza sets up a dialogue between the poet and the patient who has undergone a face lift. The first two and a half lines, beginning with the pronoun 'You', indicate that the poet is presenting the patient's experience as told to her, more or less in the form of a conversation. Plath does not use this kind of narration anywhere else in her poetry, suggesting that she was, at that time, feeling for a way into retelling an experience through a second person.

- Compare the use of the second-person pronoun here with that in 'Lesbos' (pp.55–7).

After the caesura in the third line, indicated by the colon, the account becomes that of a first-person, 'I', narrator who is telling her own story. It is evident immediately from the recording poet that the patient/speaker has undergone a face lift when we are told that she is 'exhibiting the tight white/Mummy-cloths' that swaddle her face. When the speaker begins her own narration she tells us that 'When I was nine', anaesthesia was an unpleasant sensation – 'banana gas through a frog-mask' – that led to nausea and bad dreams. The second stanza shows that now, though, the administration of an anaesthetic is much simpler and less disturbing, adding to the sensation that a kind of rebirth is taking place.

The experience is almost couched in terms of an adventure as the speaker is 'Traveling/Nude as Cleopatra', the historical reference linking to the suggestion in the third stanza of the possibility of growing 'backward', at least into a new body. A light-hearted, faintly mocking mood is established in the second stanza with the almost rollicking movement of the speaker, 'Fizzy with sedatives and unusually humorous/I roll to an anteroom'; this is the adventure, the beginning of the process of change or rebirth, yet 'something precious', possibly the old self, 'Is leaking from the finger-vents'. And then, with the apt simile 'Darkness wipes me out like chalk on a blackboard', we recognise that the moment has come for a dramatic metamorphosis to begin.

In the 'five days I lie in secret', the speaker feels old age 'draining' away 'into my pillow' as the secretive process of renewal takes place. In this third stanza she recounts the details of the change as skin 'peels away easy as paper', the simile of the peeling away and the skin tightening becoming almost a tactile sensation for readers. The transformation now takes place in earnest as the speaker 'grow[s] backward' into herself as a young married woman.

As in many of Plath's poems, the 'mirror' is a device that reflects ageing (see the earlier discussion of 'Mirror'). Here the older woman's image is changing; the 'sagg[ing]' lines in her 'Old sock-face', symbolic of her ageing self, have been 'trapped' and put in a 'laboratory jar' to 'wither' away while she wakes 'Pink and smooth as a baby', transfigured into a younger woman. The ageing woman has given birth to her younger self and is, therefore, a 'Mother to myself'.

Although the poet has set up a kind of interview with the patient as a narrative strategy, there is no further dialogue between them. Further, the ironic tone that is maintained throughout suggests that Plath mocks the idea of mere renovation through plastic surgery, believing, perhaps, that renewal or self-knowledge must be hard won and is not attainable simply through the 'peel[ing]' off of facial skin. This idea is further accentuated by the statement that 'Skin doesn't have roots', implying the old adage that 'skin deep' is only a superficial change and not deep or permanent.

Although we do not come to know the speaker/character beyond the incident of the face lift, the narration strategy is successful in presenting Plath's central and continuing theme of rebirth. The tone of mockery and playfulness tells us more about the poet's attitude to plastic surgery, or indeed to her subject, than it does about the speaker herself. The impression we gain of the patient's character shows only that she is an optimist who is rather pleased with her deception, of even her 'best friend'. She is secretive and vain, yet it is clear that her youthful mien does not convince the observer of her ability to vanquish old age.

First-person narrative voice in 'Tulips'

Written after an appendectomy that followed a miscarriage, 'Tulips' (pp.24–6) is set in a hospital environment similar to 'Face Lift'. Here Plath uses those personal experiences to express the complex emotions that attend the loss of a child through miscarriage where grief eventually gives way to the recognition that life goes on. The first-person singular speaker/persona of 'Tulips' allows her thoughts to extend beyond the confines of the hospital and her inert situation, as the tulips evoke thoughts of both birth and death. The helplessness that she feels, having relinquished all personal responsibility and given herself over wholly to the ministrations of the hospital staff – 'I have given my name and my day-clothes up to the nurses/And my history to the anesthetist and my body to surgeons' – is contrasted with the activity of her thought processes. And in these silent 'white' and antiseptic surroundings the red of the tulips is an intrusion, symbolic of the energy of the world outside, which the speaker has eschewed as she ponders the purity that death brings.

Key point

'Tulips' is crafted in such a way as to create a pattern so that the speaker's thoughts descend from life into death and then ascend from death into life.

The images of numbness and anaesthetised 'peacefulness' of the first four stanzas are reversed in the last four as the patient, who begins at a point where she has given up her identity – 'I am nobody' – reclaims it through the instrument of the red tulips. The 'too excitable' tulips and their 'explosions' of colour signify being in the first stanza and 'love' in the last, as the speaker comes to accept her return to life, 'aware of [her] heart'. In the central stanza the speaker reaches the point of renunciating life. She 'only wanted/To lie with my hands turned up and be utterly empty', feeling that only in death can she achieve the freedom from care, and the peace she desires.

The 'winter' images of coldness and whiteness, the 'snowed-in' atmosphere of the first stanza, signify the hospital environment and represent all that imprisons her in her own existence. The speaker feels a sense of dismemberment in the second stanza – 'They have propped my head between the pillow and the sheet-cuff' – as she becomes merely a 'head', an 'eye', disconnected from the business around her as the 'nurses pass and pass … the way gulls pass'. In the third stanza her body becomes, metaphorically, 'a pebble', smoothed over by the medical staff. As is usual in Plath, the recurring image of a stone symbolises a reduction to the core, the mind and body stripped of all pretence and human 'associations', the low point from which a gradual ascent is eventually possible. Having renounced all feeling, she does not need 'baggage', neither the literal baggage of her 'overnight case' nor the emotional baggage of 'husband and child'. She is 'sick of' their dependence on her, of their 'little smiling hooks' that anchor her.

At the fifth line of the fourth stanza, the tense shifts from present to past tense as the speaker recalls that the anaesthesia provided a moment when she was able to cast off her 'teaset', 'bureaus of linen' and 'books'. As 'the water went over my head', she drowned. Then the tense changes back to the present as she remembers it as a moment of purification – 'I have never been so pure' – that now allows her to assess her life as a 'thirty-year-old cargo boat', stripped but 'peaceful' and 'utterly empty'. But she cannot give in to the final peacefulness of death, and the flowers that she 'didn't want' prompt her to turn towards life again.

After the first line – 'The tulips are too excitable' – the personified tulips do not appear again until the sixth stanza when they intrude upon the speaker as a painful reminder of the life she wants consciously to reject. Set against the whiteness of the background, the redness of the tulips is an affront. They 'hurt me', but their breathing through their wrapping – 'white swaddlings' – signifies life. Their 'redness … corresponds' to the redness of her 'wound' and they subtly remind her that she is alive, even though they 'weigh' her down and upset her 'with their sudden tongues and their color'. They now 'watch' her, preventing her attempts at effacement as 'a cut-paper shadow'. She wants to reject their 'vivid[ness]', their intruding into her world, 'eat[ing]' her 'oxygen' like wild and 'dangerous' predators, but she cannot.

The rhythm of the poem accelerates in the last two stanzas as now the tulips 'concentrate' the attention of the speaker and she must commit herself to life. They are the bearers only of noise in the eighth stanza, but they bring warmth in the final stanza. Through them the speaker becomes 'aware' of her heart, which opens and closes its bowl of red blooms (pumping life-giving blood around her body) out of 'sheer love' of her. The water no longer runs over her as 'a pebble' but is 'like the sea' that is the source of all life. The poem ends with the speaker's tentative recognition that the 'country far away as health' is the world that she must embrace once more.

The melancholy tone of the first half of the poem gives way if not to joy, then certainly to the possibility of some kind of harmony that comes with the acceptance that life is warmth and that the heart is not easily stilled. Unlike the patient in 'Face Lift', the speaker is shown to be overcoming great personal depression that leaves her seeking the peacefulness that death seems to offer, until the 'explosion' of the tulips brings a vitality that allows her to rise above the depression. Aside from the mood of the speaker, though, we learn very little about her personality or character.

- This poem is made up of nine seven-line stanzas, each one a separate unit, without the device of the run-on line between verses that Plath so often uses. The end-stopped verses heighten the effect of the packaging of time into distinct units of the hospital day.
- The descending/ascending movement of the poem demonstrates the control Plath mastered in her later poems.
- There is an abundance of poetic devices here. Note, in particular, the way the tulips are variously described: 'like dangerous animals'; 'like the mouth of some great African cat' (similes); 'A dozen red lead sinkers' (metaphor).

As Plath became surer of her poetic control she continued to utilise the device of a first-person singular speaker until her final poems, 'Contusion' and 'Edge' (p.77), in which she attempts a distancing through the use of a third-person, omniscient narrator. Through the first-person speaker she is able to portray an immediacy to, and a connection with, the reader that the more remote third-person device cannot achieve.

If we compare the earlier poem 'Spinster' (pp.4–5), which is a straight narrative using omniscient narration, with the two poems above, the difference in narrative voice becomes obvious.

Third-person observer in 'Spinster'

A tale of rejected love, 'Spinster' uses the voice of a third-person observer whose view is that there is a violence in love that threatens the calm of women. The woman in the story starts by being 'intolerably struck' by overwhelming emotions of love, described negatively as 'birds' irregular babel', 'leaves' litter' (note the alliteration) and 'tumult'. Further, her lover's 'gestures' of love 'unbalance the air' as the fertility associated with a relationship – 'a rank wilderness of fern and flower' (more alliteration) – is reflected in her mind as the season's 'disarray'.

The spinster wishes, then, in the third stanza, for the 'austere' winter to bring the 'heart's frosty discipline' away from the 'afflict[ion]' of these burgeoning feelings of love that threaten to overpower the senses. The harshness of winter's 'white and black/Ice and rock' is contrasted with the giddy sensations of love as the observer sees the spinster withdrawing to keep 'each sentiment within [a] border'. The fourth stanza returns to a description using extremes of vocabulary to describe the uproar of her senses: 'Unruly enough to pitch her five queenly wits'; the woman's five senses are overridden by 'vulgar motley'. Finally, Plath uses hyperbole to describe love as 'treason' as the spinster withdraws 'neatly' from the 'tumult'. In the final stanza she vows never to become so 'afflicted' again.

The spinster's characteristics are only sketchily conveyed to us through the omniscient narrator from whom we learn that the subject is a young woman – 'girl' – who appears to become slightly hysterical at the prospect of love, or at least at the unsettling effects the emotion brings. As a result she withdraws from life behind a 'barricade', holding off her fears. She rejects not only the disorder that love brings but also her own fertility, and by avoiding experience she can control it. In deciding not to become a victim of her emotions, or of her lover's, she eschews life itself.

Instead of a first-person speaker being able to convey her own feelings, the omniscient narrator relies on description alone and, thus, readers must react to the forcefulness of the language for the point to be hammered home. This is in marked contrast to the subtlety of the language in a poem such as 'Tulips' where readers are privy to the speaker's thoughts and feelings. The exaggeration of the vocabulary (hyperbole) and the repetition of devices such as alliteration, contribute to this assessment.

Although the tone seems playful, Plath might be suggesting in 'Spinster', written in the year of her marriage, that love brings disorder to a woman's life. It is an early declaration of her dilemma that married life and love impinge on her professional writing and that women, in particular, are disadvantaged by marriage in that way. This poem, though written using the third-person narrative voice, shows that in comparison with poems such as 'Tulips', Plath's later adoption of first-person narration is more successful. The 'I' persona brings to her readers a more powerful communication of emotions, thoughts and experiences, and establishes the tone instantly.

First-person plural narrative voice in 'The Babysitters'

- The narrative strategy in 'The Babysitters' (pp.35–7) is a variation from both first-person singular and omniscient narration to the use of first-person plural narration. Here Plath tells a tale of two sisters who shared much but are now separated by time and geography.

- Compare the narrative strategy in this poem with that in others. How effective is it? Why do you think Plath did not use first-person plural narration in other poems?
- What tone does the narrator use and how does it change through the poem?

Characters

The characters in Plath's poems are portrayed obliquely; she uses them only to convey a central idea. In short poems it is not possible to achieve the same in-depth characterisation that is possible in prose fiction, plays or film texts. Nevertheless, Plath's speakers are the bearers of her central concerns about the human condition and, more particularly, about women in a world that is not only dominated by men but where even the lexicon of poetry is male-oriented.

THEMES & ISSUES

It is evident throughout Plath's poems that each one forms part of a loose sequence of recurring symbols and ideas. The issues she raises emerge from the images, and are rarely clearly stated. Moreover, since her concerns are embedded in the images they cannot easily be separated but, instead, can merely be grouped together. For instance, Plath's interest in the search for identity overlaps with ideas of motherhood, pain and loss so that each poem forms a part of her overall beliefs regarding life itself and the place of death within life.

The possibility of personal growth

As we have seen already, Plath is interested in the possibility of rebirth, not in the sense of reincarnation, but as a process of entering into a new phase or a further development, perhaps, towards maturity. This idea is often associated with hospitalisation, such as in 'Face Lift' (pp.21–2) and 'Tulips' (pp.24–6): works that show, in different ways, Plath investigating the opportunity of casting off the old self and acquiring a new one.

'The Stones'

Plath suggests that the attainment of self-knowledge is a painful process. From the long sequence 'Poem for a Birthday', 'The Stones' (pp.16–17) is an early investigation into the possibility of rebirth. Reputed to be modelled on her recovery from her first suicide attempt, again Plath establishes a hospital setting – 'This is the city where men are mended' – where, through surrealist images, a patient comes to a painful acceptance that she is once more part of the world of the living. Plath, however, is not writing a poetic autobiography but, rather, is using her own personal experience in a much more inclusive dramatic structure to show that the very experience of pain is the means by which we achieve personal growth.

The title of the poem keys us into a recurring image: that of the pebble or stone. This represents a stripping down to the nucleus where there is no facade to deceive oneself about anything beyond the inner self. The speaker records that she 'lie[s] on a great anvil', a hospital bed where she will undergo a cure after her near death by suicide – 'When I fell out of the light'. She has been pummelled as by a 'pestle', becoming 'a still pebble' stripped of all emotion and association. But life is still there – 'the mouth-hole piped out' – and the stages of her rebirth follow.

Through the silence, she is revived and a slow recovery ensues as she 'suck[s] at the paps of darkness'. She is fed as 'one stone eye' (note the play on 'I' here) opens and she 'see[s] the light'; her hearing also begins to function – 'A wind unstoppers the chamber/Of the ear'. She takes in life-giving water but as daylight comes, it is evident that this is not a joyful birth, but rather a reluctant rebirth where the world is recognised and seen as unwelcome. Nevertheless, the process continues as the torturers – 'grafters' – begin the shock treatment that will effect some kind of cure. The images here are shocking, as they are meant to be: heated 'pincers', 'delicate hammers' and 'A current agitates the wires/ Volt upon volt'. By stanza eleven, the images represent renewal and the wholeness to come, for 'The storerooms are full of hearts' and 'This is the city of spare parts' where the body can be made whole once more. In stanza twelve a vague note of hope is struck with the introduction of 'children' that symbolise new and continuing life.

The last two stanzas outline that 'Love' is as delicate as a 'rose' and so the body has been mended, like a broken 'vase' is 'reconstructed'. The last two lines strike a note of sombre irony as 'My mendings itch. There is nothing to do./I shall be as good as new'. There is no tone of desperation, however; rather, the speaker's mood is one of resignation. Despite her recovery, there is a sense of diminution and numbness because, of course, she cannot be as good as new. She can, however, use her experience to rebuild her life.

Key point

Plath shows in 'The Stones', and in many other poems, that only in rebirth can the true self exist in its ideal form.

Personal growth and the father figure

Plath's exploration of the theme of rebirth and the search for personal growth is evident in all the poems that involve a father figure. The poems 'Full Fathom Five', 'Little Fugue' and 'Daddy' can be seen as forming a loose sequence within a larger one, where Plath pursues an idea that the lost father hinders the development of the daughter into mature adulthood. 'Full Fathom Five'[16] shows the speaker/daughter grappling with the image of a drowned, Neptune-bearded father who is elusive and yet she is caught in his 'labyrinthine tangle'. The images of the father, near and yet remote – 'You float near/As keeled ice-mountains' – make communication impossible; Plath uses the sea as a central metaphor for a childhood bereft of a real father who, as a result, is projected as a 'god'. She cannot reach him because he inhabits the sea, whereas she is left on the shore – 'I walk dry on your kingdom's border' – while imagining that through death – 'I would breathe water' – she can at last reach out to him.

Of the background to this poem Plath wrote in her journal:

> It relates more richly to my life and imagery than anything else I've dreamed up: has the background of *The Tempest*, the association of the sea, which is a central metaphor for my childhood, my poems and the artist's subconscious, of the father image – relating to my own father, the buried male muse and god-creator risen to be my mate in Ted, to the sea-father Neptune.[17]

[16] The title is taken from a line in Shakespeare's *The Tempest*: 'Full fathom five thy father lies' (Act 1, scene 2, line 399).

[17] *Journals*, 11 May 1958, pp.222–3.

She goes on to quote James Joyce: '"and it's old and old it's sad and old it's sad and weary I go back to you my cold father, my cold mad father, my cold mad feary father" – so the river flows to the paternal source of godhead'.[18] These excerpts show the process of her thought patterns as Plath strives to craft her central ideas into poems.

A variation of the overt images of rebirth as seen in 'Face Lift', 'Tulips' and 'The Stones' is offered in 'Daddy'. The poem shows Plath continuing to refine her symbolism of rebirth through the daughter–father relationship. In order for the female speaker to achieve emotional maturity she must divest herself of a self-constructed father figure who has dominated her life, preventing her from growing up. As well as being central to 'Full Fathom Five', the daughter–father relationship is explored in 'Little Fugue' (pp.38–9), which is a forerunner of 'Daddy'. In all these poems, Plath presents her readers with the idea of failed communication between father and daughter being an impediment to the daughter's personal growth.

The yew tree, a phallic symbol Plath used earlier in 'The Moon and the Yew Tree' (see the earlier section on 'Symbolism of the yew tree'), appears again in 'Little Fugue' to signal male dominance. Its blackness is contrasted with the whiteness of the clouds above it – 'The yew's black fingers wag;/Cold clouds go over' – suggesting that black and white are colours far removed from each other, like the daughter is from her father. There is no possible communication between the 'deaf', the 'dumb' and the 'blind', signifying the speaker/daughter's despair at not being able to reach her dead father: 'Gothic and barbarous', he was 'A yew hedge of orders'. He is 'pure German' and the idea of the impossibility of dialogue between them is reiterated in the repetition of 'silence'. The father died – 'Death opened' – when the daughter 'was seven' and she has continued to 'survive' in desolation at his absence.

The daughter/speaker, however, rebels against her absent father in 'Daddy' (pp.52–4). The poem is the speaker's act of exorcism to expel the fantasy father she has constructed in childhood and that has left

[18] *Journals*, 11 May 1958, p.223.

her subjugated in adulthood. The colour black acts as a connecting image: the father is represented as a 'black shoe', which is similar to the way in which men in 'The Munich Mannequins' are symbolised as 'shoes'. The daughter has 'lived like a foot' that has been forced into the father's shoes. This image suggests that she is trapped by her father, his personality and his history, and it is reinforced by an analogous image of the Jews being ground down under the Nazi foot – 'The boot in the face'. Plath is suggesting that the daughter is both 'a Jew' and a Nazi, as she has inherited her father's genes. This brings about her emotional paralysis. Continuing the black imagery, Daddy the 'panzer man' is also represented as a 'black' 'swastika' and as the 'black man' who bit her 'pretty red heart in two' when he betrayed her by dying. Now she is 'finally through', the 'black telephone' representing the impossibility of connection.

There are parallel ideas working together in this poem. The girl is dominated by the father/persona she has created in childhood. She seeks release from the numbness that prevents her from attaining emotional fulfilment in adulthood. The very title indicates that this is a childish dependence. At the same time, the historical references to the Holocaust both assist in presenting her dilemma and also reflect Plath's own geopolitical concerns. For example, her inherited genetic sequences of Nazi and Jew prevent her from speaking. She is intimidated – 'I could never talk to you./The tongue stuck in my jaw' – which parallels the Holocaust experience of the Jews 'stuck in a barb wire snare', suggesting the Jewish persecution and terror. Both daughter and prisoner are unable to escape, so the child before its father and the Jew before the Nazi are impotent.

Plath manipulates her persona into confronting the demon that has possessed her and that she must exorcise. The child's simple perspective is grounded in the baby language and nursery rhyme rhythm of the poem. Words such as 'gobbledygoo' and 'Achoo' reflect a child's view. But with the emphatic 'Daddy, I have had to kill you', the speaker begins to catalogue the father's omissions before the final rejection. The tone becomes one of confrontation. First, he has been in her life only like a 'Marble-heavy' inanimate statue. The third stanza places his head in the sea as a part-Neptune figure, unrecoverable for the daughter as he is in 'Full Fathom Five'. Then he is a German Nazi, a fascist who has ruled the speaker's life. Finally, he is a torturer with 'a love of the rack and the screw', and a 'vampire', melded into the husband who has also betrayed her.

In the thirteenth stanza she 'made a model' of him, suggesting that the constructed image of her father, in effect an effigy, had also served as a prototype for all men, including the husband to whom she said 'I do, I do'. Therefore, she must destroy both the image and the effigy of the 'man in black with a Meinkampf look' in order to free herself of the magic that enthrals her. She is reborn when 'they stuck me together with glue' in an act of remodelling that permits her ultimate rejection of her own constructed fantasy. With the emphatic ending 'Daddy, daddy, you bastard, I'm through', the woman is able, at last, to control her childish phantom and stands at the point where personal growth is possible.

- The sixteen verses of five lines each are written in a powerful nursery-rhyme rhythm. The stanzas have an irregular pattern of rhyme, but with one dominant rhyme throughout. Forty-one of the eighty lines repeat the same rhyme: you/do/shoe/Jew/blue/screw and so on. The effect of this is to create an impression of great speed and furious energy.

The search for a sense of identity: 'Ariel'

Through images of mirrors, reflections, stones and hooks, it is clear that Plath is searching for a sense of identity. She found it in 'Ariel' (pp.62–3).[19] Her persona is a young woman going for a ride on her favourite horse, but the ride is much more than this. This is a poem of the senses where we see, hear, touch and taste as the horse's body and the rider's merge.

[19] The title refers to 'Ariel's Song' in Shakespeare's *The Tempest* (act 1, scene 2). Note that Ariel is a power for freedom and good throughout the play. Ariel was also the name of Plath's horse. In addition, in the Bible, Isaiah 29, Jerusalem is referred to as Ariel, the city destined to be destroyed by fire.

With the final unity between horse and rider, it is an act of liberation, the culmination of a journey towards the centre of life and, perhaps, even death. The poem is wholly positive as the speaker moves from stillness – 'Stasis in darkness' – towards the light at the end in a powerful suggestion that the speaker/poet has reached a pinnacle of achievement.

The horse emerges from the 'darkness' of the pale light of morning – 'the substanceless blue'. The sun is beginning to rise as the horse (Ariel) gallops across the countryside – 'Pivot of heels and knees!' – while the rider tries to catch 'The brown arc/Of the neck' and is clawed at by the blackberries – 'Nigger-eye/Berries' that 'cast dark/Hooks' – on the side of the road. She does not stop to taste them, however, as she is propelled forward with the horse. As the two entities merge, the speaker hears her own cry as if it were that of the child within and flies towards the burning sunrise – 'the red/Eye, the cauldron of morning'. The physical and psychological aspects of the self come together in a ride into illumination; she sees the light, as she becomes naked both physically and emotionally – 'White/Godiva, I unpeel –/Dead hands, dead stringencies' – and finds freedom in the physical act of unpeeling. She has discarded the restrictions that threaten her creativity.

The poem draws us into its beautiful cosmos. As the pace of the horse quickens, the intensity of the visual effects becomes greater. Plath's metaphors suggest a fusion between disparate objects, as in the lines 'I/Foam to wheat, a glitter of seas'. The ride across the meadows suddenly becomes an ocean voyage. The speaker merges with the sun as the reader becomes one with her. If she is to be destroyed in the cauldron of energy, the sun, the reader is enticed into a kind of death as well, a spirit of abandonment. For the speaker, this flying into the sun becomes an act of purification that allows her an ultimate sense of identity. The speaker must transform herself into something powerful to make this journey; she becomes an 'arrow', a phallic symbol, the ultimate symbol of masculine power. Thus she is not a sacrificial victim because, as a masculine arrow, she absorbs the power of the sun; she is the spirit that becomes whole through the purifying fire of the sun.

The speaker of the poem is fully aware that her desire for the power she has claimed for herself might be destructive, for she refers to her journey as 'Suicidal'. The unclothed body suggests the vulnerability of the female, for although she has assumed the arrogance of the male, she is still naked and exposed – yet there is a sense of liberation, as if this is the only way that she can find the self within. Finally, this act of riding suggests the ecstasy of physical motion that becomes the creative energy that sustains the speaker/poet. Like Shakespeare's Ariel, Plath's speaker finds freedom at the end as she reaches a point of great depth of feeling and insight, a kind of metamorphosis that can only be read as a triumphant affirmation.

Competing roles of women

What we hear in each of Plath's poems is a strong voice, one of many voices that often conflict with one another. These competing voices suggest that we cannot be all things at all times – just as a 'smart girl' cannot have 'everything she wants'[20] – and this forms the central dramatic thought and feeling. These voices equate to roles that provide a dissonant tension within each poem, as we have already seen in poems such as 'Daddy'.

Daughter

Plath had an uneasy relationship with her mother and writes in her journal:

> I never knew the love of a father ... after the age of eight ... the only man who'd love me steady through life: she came in one morning with tears ... in her eyes and told me he was gone for good. I hate her for that ... He was an ogre. But I miss him. He was old, but she married an old man to be my father. It was her fault.[21]

[20] *Journals*, 12 December 1958, pp.266–7.

[21] *Journals*, 12 December 1958, p.267.

It is this parental conflict that Plath often dramatises in her poems.

As we have seen in 'Daddy', Plath explores the daughter/father relationship. The tension in this relationship is encapsulated in the lines:

> I was ten when they buried you.
> At twenty I tried to die
> And get back, back, back to you.

- A poem most explicitly concerned with a daughter–father relationship is 'Electra on Azalea Path' (in *The Collected Poems*).
- Plath explores the conflict in the mother/daughter role in the poem 'Medusa' (in *The Collected Poems*) and her novel *The Bell Jar*.

Wife

Plath clearly understood the conflict that beset women in the 1950s, and her poems still resonate today. In her journals she records that she is happy that her husband 'shows his gladness for what I cook him and joy for when I make something, a poem or a cake'[22], as if the making of a cake could ever equate to the creative input needed to make a poem. Men, however, often do trivialise working women, even today, implying that their work must be subordinated to the their needs or suggesting that women should work only part-time. This is still true in the twenty-first century in some relationships where women continue to be pressured to juggle the conflicting roles of having a career and being a wife, mother and housekeeper.

Plath records:

> I needed ... a man who would make a perfect circuit of love and all else with me ... the only man I could love ... do what he wanted in this world, and want to cook for and bear children for and write with.[23]

---

[22] *Journals*, 12 December 1958, p.269.
[23] *Journals*, 12 December 1958, p.269.

But she also expresses her fear of being dominated by her husband, wondering: 'How to develop my independence? Not tell him everything … not leading outer life'.[24] This is the female dilemma that men are rarely bothered by – the need to have an independent, creative life while, at the same time, fulfilling the dual role of feminine creativity, being a loving wife and mother.

The tension between the roles of wife and husband is evident in 'Tulips' (analysed in 'Narrative voices') where the hospital patient speaker declares she is 'sick of baggage' (p.24). This is both the literal baggage – 'My patent leather overnight case' – and the emotional baggage of husband and children described in most negative terms as 'My husband and child smiling out of the family photo;/Their smiles catch onto my skin, little smiling hooks'. The 'hooks' represent the familial bonds that imprison her, limiting her creativity by their very existence.

In 'Daddy', the speaker kills off the husband at the same time as she exorcises the father figure: 'And I said I do, I do … If I've killed one man, I've killed two –/The vampire who said he was you' (p.54). In her journals Plath records that she identifies Hughes with her father 'at certain times', afraid that his lack of sexual fidelity equates to her father's desertion of her when he died.[25] In 'Daddy' this idea has been poeticised and made universal.

'Lesbos'[26] (pp.55–7) examines a hostile relationship between two women. Their husbands are spoken of in derogatory terms that reflect the speaker's true feelings towards them and indict them for her own untenable situation. The narrative structure is such that the speaker talks directly to the other woman and she is angry. The domestic situation between the two is one of conflict that has a tone of credibility as the speaker hurls accusations at the other and seems to blame her for her own situation. She asserts that: 'You say your husband is just no good

[24] *Journals*, 26 December 1958, p.277.

[25] *Journals*, 27 December 1958, p.278.

[26] The title of the poem is ironic, as Lesbos was the centre of female intellectual activity in ancient Greece.

to you./His Jew-Mama guards his sweet sex like a pearl' and then, 'The impotent husband slumps out for a coffee./I try to keep him in', and further down, 'A dog picked up your doggy husband. He went on' but finally: 'Now I am silent, hate/Up to my neck'. The hate she transmits to readers is almost palpable; it is despair born of hopelessness as she is tied down 'doped and thick from my last sleeping pill' amongst 'a stink of fat and baby crap'.

The rift between the two women is obvious, but it is for the husband that the speaker reserves her true invective. She packs almost in a trance:

> I am packing the hard potatoes like good clothes,
> I am packing the babies,
> I am packing the sick cats

The repetition reinforces the mechanical action of a woman at the end of her tether. She recognises that her enforced departure is caused by the complexity of the roles that they both must perform, but more particularly the husband is the problem as she accuses the other woman of not really recognising the cause: 'You know who you hate./He is hugging his ball and chain down by the gate ... Every day you fill him with soul-stuff, like a pitcher./You are so exhausted'. The other woman is lost because she cannot admit the cause of her own hopelessness and the speaker's tone is disparaging as she leaves – 'I see your cute décor/Close on you'. Disgusted, the speaker knows there can be no reconciliation between the women as she pretends to gloss over their quarrel – 'I say I may be back./You know what lies are for'.

- The flowing narrative, here, is masterly as Plath manages to convince readers of the drama's realism. A pattern of sound underpins the structure; the dominant sounds are s/z ones that create an effect of hissing, of breath being held back and escaping through clenched teeth.
- In two other late poems, 'Purdah' and 'Lady Lazarus', Plath uses characters who rise above their anguish and exact retribution for their pain upon men. (These are in *The Collected Poems*.)

Mother

Plath's attitude to motherhood is ambiguous, as we have seen in 'The Manor Garden' and 'Morning Song' where the mother feels vulnerable and somewhat bemused by the enormity of her responsibility for the new baby. The image of the 'fat gold watch', which can be interpreted variously, is nevertheless repulsive, but it is in 'Lesbos' (pp.55–7) that the mother's role is most carefully examined. The speaker's young daughter is having a tantrum, screaming 'face down on the floor', while the 'fat snail' of a baby sits on the 'orange linoleum'. The speaker details, with bitter irony, the advice given by the other woman, the 'you' of the poem, as to what she should do – 'I should wear tiger pants, I should have an affair'[27] – but this catalogue of hate is located in the suggestion of the mother/speaker's inability to combine her various female roles. The other woman has nothing but disdain for the speaker's daughter, calling her a 'bastard', yet she coos over the younger one simply because he is a boy.

If the speaker is not coping with motherhood, then the 'you' persona has never come to terms with managing her roles of wife, mother and friend. There is no communication between these two mothers, who ought to be united in their wretchedness. The 'you' mother loves male children even while loathing the male adult who is her husband. Further, she discriminates against the female child, has 'blown [her] tubes like a bad radio/Clear of voices and history', and in 'The smog of cooking, the smog of hell' these two mothers are 'two venomous opposites'.

'Nick and the Candlestick' (p.65), however, has a beautiful rendering of the mother's role. The poem stems from the imaginative associations of a mother nursing her child by candlelight and her concern for the potential dangers of the world that he must negotiate. There is a note of melancholy in the first half of the poem as the speaker contrasts the complexities of adulthood with the purity and innocence of infancy. The candlelight is used as the organising principle of the poem, the first stanza

[27] Note here the echoes of TS Eliot's poem, 'The Love Song of J. Alfred Prufrock' (1917).

setting the scene of the mother and child in candlelight as the 'Waxy stalactites/Drip and thicken'. The harsh imagery of 'Cold homicides', 'icicles', a 'vice of knives' and a 'piranha' follow, enumerating the threats to the baby. But in stanza seven the tone changes to one of maternal softness as the 'yellows' of the candlelight 'hearten' her to ask the ultimate question for all mothers: 'O love, how did you get here?' She remembers the feeling of the baby inside, his 'crossed position' and the 'ruby' flow of his 'blood' that 'blooms clean', symbolising his innocence. 'The pain' of the world that he 'wake[s] to' is not of his contriving, and to protect him the mother/speaker has 'hung our cave with roses,/With soft rugs' to comfort and protect him. The beauty of the last verse – 'You are the one/Solid the spaces lean on, envious./You are the baby in the barn' – affirms the mother's love for the child and conjures up a picture of the baby Jesus. But the joy of the ending does not evade the pain of the first half for, despite the warmth of the cave hung with 'roses', neither baby nor mother can escape the 'mercuric/Atoms' that 'drip/Into the terrible well'.

In her motherhood poems, Plath's speakers run the full gamut of conflicting feelings both towards their role and towards the children themselves. It is a tribute to her poetics, though, that she could create the harmony of the mother and child relationship in the last stanza of 'Nick and the Candlestick'.

Artist

In her journals Plath records that

> Writing is a religious act: it is an ordering, a reforming, a relearning and reloving of people and the world as they are and as they might be. A shaping which does not pass away like a day of typing … The writing lasts: it goes about on its own in the world … The worst thing, worse than all of them would be to live with not writing.[28]

[28] *Journals*, 12 December 1958, p.271.

Even from an early age Plath was sustained by writing, but at times her poetry makes a link between sterility and writer's block. 'The Munich Mannequins' begins with the line 'Perfection is terrible, it cannot have children' (p.74). What follows is a series of images of desolation, coldness, loneliness and silence, and, more particularly, the ambiguous image of menstruation that represents both barrenness (in the sense that conception has not taken place) and the blood flow of creativity. This suggests that Plath felt childbearing and writing were antithetical to each other and in trying to balance these different parts of her life she was striving for perfection. Clearly, the birth of a child signifies a period of inactivity for a woman writer and this meant frustration and depression for Plath, sometimes leading to her inability to write at all for periods of time.

It is in the spareness of one of her last poems, 'Words' (p.76), that Plath was able to articulate strongly her sense of powerlessness as a poet to change anything with mere words. The four short stanzas are a striking expression of the impotence the poet/speaker feels: her sense that words are not enough. In the first stanza we hear the ring of axes as the words strike and echo, but by the end the poet's words become 'dry and riderless', as if they are no longer connected to the poet/speaker herself – she 'Encounter[s] them on the road'. The link between self and language has been severed; there is only destiny in the form of the fixed stars that 'From the bottom of the pool .../Govern a life'.

It is this ability to universalise the creative experience that marks Plath as a successful poet. She takes her own experience as a writer, mother, daughter and wife and articulates the frustration of the conflict between the feminine roles women are expected to manipulate, turning it into art. For her, the sap did well 'like tears' as she wrestled with life itself, but she shaped in words her finely wrought experiences to help us understand not just Plath herself, but our own place in the world.

QUESTIONS & ANSWERS

This section focuses on your own analytical writing on the text, and gives you strategies for producing high-quality responses in your coursework and exam essays.

Essay topics

1 How difficult is it for Plath's female speakers to manage the often conflicting roles of daughter and mother, wife and artist?

2 In what ways do Plath's speakers show their vulnerability in surviving the pressures of daily life?

3 "The blood flood is the flood of love,/The absolute sacrifice." ('The Munich Manequins')
What is it that Plath's tragic heroines sacrifice?

4 "Fire smelted his eyes to lumps/Of pale blue vitreous stuff, opaque …" ('The Burnt-out Spa')
How does Plath use images of opacity to indicate our inability to see ourselves as we really are?

5 "I see myself, flat, ridiculous, a cut-paper shadow …" ('Tulips')
How does Plath use images of effacement to show that we are all searching for a better person inside ourselves?

6 'Through images of terror and war, Plath suggests that our lives are hopelessly threatened by outside forces.'
Discuss.

7 "I simply cannot see where there is to get to." ('The Moon and the Yew Tree')
How is this world view conveyed by Sylvia Plath's poems?

8 "I am silver and exact." ('Mirror')
'The poems suggest that although we fear what we see in the mirror, we are fundamentally searching for our true identity.'
Discuss.

9 'Plath's poetry shows that individuals often need to hide their pain from those around them.'
Discuss.

10 "From the bottom of the pool, fixed stars/Govern a life." ('Words')
'Plath's poems show that our lives are governed by destiny.'
To what extent do you agree?

Analysing a sample topic

How difficult is it for Plath's female speakers to manage the often conflicting female roles of daughter and mother, wife and artist?

- This topic asks you to look at the speakers who combine the roles of wife and mother. Inherent in a discussion of this would be the drama that arises from the conflicting roles the speaker is asked to play.
- Decide which poems will best suit the topic; consider those such as 'Lesbos' and 'Morning Song' where the mother feels ambivalent about her role as parent, and 'Daddy' where the speaker 'kills' her father.
- Begin by examining the key words in the topic such as 'often conflicting' and 'female roles'. You might want to suggest a counter-argument that these roles are also fulfilling ones that are not in conflict.
- In your introduction make it clear what strategies you will employ to address the topic. Begin with a strong opening that creates a frame for the discussion that is to follow. Include your main ideas.
- The first paragraph should address the topic widely. Begin with a good topic sentence that indicates the points to be discussed. Keep to one idea in each paragraph and support your statements with evidence from the text. By selecting one poem for discussion first, you can set up a 'compare and contrast' method that is effective in discussing different feminine roles.

- In your next paragraph, use another poem for contrast. Linking phrases such as 'on the other hand' or 'unlike' are useful when moving between poems. In this way you can set up another group of ideas for discussion. Remember to keep the topic in mind and make effective links between paragraphs. One way of doing this is by using a key word from the last sentence of one paragraph in the first sentence of the next.
- Use short quotations and weave them through your own words.
- Including key words from the topic ensures you keep the discussion on track.
- Your conclusion should sum up your ideas. It is a good ploy to make some grand statements about female roles and the conflict that can arise. Reiterating the terms of the topic is a good way of showing that you have developed a sustained argument within the parameters of the topic.

SAMPLE ANSWER

"The blood flood is the flood of love/The absolute sacrifice."
('The Munich Mannequins')
What is it that Plath's female characters sacrifice?

In many of Sylvia Plath's poems, sacrifice is an inherent aspect of women's lives. Those who become wives and mothers find that their independence and agency are sacrificed. On the other hand, to be deprived of love and the capacity to have children is also seen as a form of sacrifice – perhaps the 'absolute sacrifice'. Some female figures in the poems seek to sacrifice their own lives, seeking respite from the turmoil of life in the stillness of death. To do so, however, means giving up the pleasures as well as the pains of life, a sacrifice that yields no real gain.

In 'The Munich Mannequins', the inanimate female figures on display embody a version of 'perfect' womanhood: one that is perfectly unchanging and therefore barren. In this, they represent an image of femaleness that in one way signifies an ideal – a glamorous, sophisticated existence symbolised by the mannequins' slim, 'stick' figures and fur coats – but in another way signifies a profound loss. The 'absolute sacrifice' signalled by the 'blood flood' of the biologically female body is that there is no embryo; in this, the living woman and the mannequin are strangely similar. The pursuit of a fashionable beauty at the expense of motherhood means a life filled with absence, reflected in the poem by its many images of stillness and silence. People are present in this city, but in disembodied, fragmented forms: there are hands to open doors and 'broad toes' to go into shoes, but no whole human beings. Instead, the mannequins stand for a society characterised by a lack of connection between people and the inability (or refusal) to nurture new lives.

Of course, some of Plath's female speakers are mothers, and these figures also sacrifice aspects of their lives and identities. However, it is clear that such sacrifices are double-edged, as there are pleasures arising from caring for one's own child that are not otherwise accessible. In

'Morning Song', the sense of estrangement that accompanies the child's birth – 'We stand round blankly as walls' – and even the interruption of the night's sleep are compensated for by exposure to a new and fragile beauty. The baby's cry is compared to a joyful song through its 'handful of notes' and 'clear vowels' that 'rise like balloons', images of lightness and clarity contrasting with the dull heaviness of the mother-speaker as she 'stumble[s] from bed'. She has lost some of her freedom and independence, but the sacrifice of these qualities is balanced by moments of beauty and an enhanced appreciation of life.

In contrast, the woman in 'Tulips', recovering in hospital from an unspecified illness, feels that the trappings of family life are akin to 'baggage' or 'little smiling hooks'. Temporarily relieved of these responsibilities and attachments, she experiences a freedom that is almost euphoric, a peacefulness 'so big it dazes you'. The woman gains a clear sense of what it is she has lost through being a wife and a mother: a feeling of inner calm, the liberty to be 'utterly empty'. Only the gift of twelve red tulips disturbs her tranquillity, reminding her at first of the burden of her commitments but then prompting her renewed sense of her capacity to give and receive love. Her feeling of peacefulness is blissful, yet she understands it is 'what the dead close on, finally', and she ultimately chooses the passions and turbulence of life over the stillness of death.

However, the woman in 'Edge' has chosen death over life, apparently sacrificing her children at the same time. As in 'The Munich Mannequins', the notion of perfection is aligned with a state that is unchanging and lifeless, a condition in which it is impossible to create or experience love. The 'woman is perfected' in death, but it is a concept of perfection that is deeply ironic since the loss of innocent life that accompanies it is so shocking. She has a 'smile of accomplishment', yet it is clear from the poem's prevailing images of darkness and withdrawal that this woman's sacrifice represents failure rather than achievement, a sacrifice that leads not to a more fulfilled life but the complete shutting down of life's possibilities.

Absolute happiness eludes Plath's female characters; inevitably, to experience pleasure, they must give up an aspect of their lives – of their identities and freedoms. Some sacrifices, though, have a terrible cost, since they amount to a denial of life. They are made in order to achieve 'perfection', but such a state is hollow, constituted by an unchanging sameness. Conversely, the sacrifices of women who are mothers and wives are borne because of what they make possible: a strong sense of connection with others and the apprehension of beauty in the most transient, everyday encounters.

REFERENCES & READING

The text

Plath, S 1985, *Selected Poems*, chosen by Ted Hughes, Faber & Faber, London.

Further reading

Eliot, TS 1963, 'The love song of J. Alfred Prufrock' in *Collected Poems*, Harcourt Brace & Co, New York.

Hughes, T 1995, 'Interview with Ted Hughes' in *Paris Review*, Spring, available online at http://www.sylviaplath.de/plath/thint.html.

Hughes, T & McCullough, F (eds) 1991, *The Journals of Sylvia Plath*, Ballantyne Books, New York. First published in 1983.

Merwin, D, 'Vessel of wrath: a memoir of Sylvia Plath', in Stevenson, A 1989, *Bitter Fame*: *A Life of Sylvia Plath*, Houghton Mifflin, Boston.

Plath, AS (ed.) 1975, *Letters Home: Correspondence 1950–1963*, Harper & Row, New York.

Plath, S 1977, 'A comparison', in *Johnny Panic and the Bible of Dreams*, Faber & Faber, London, pp.62–5.

—— 1981, *The Collected Poems*, ed. Ted Hughes, Faber & Faber, London.

—— 1977, 'Context', in *Johnny Panic and the Bible of Dreams*, Faber & Faber, London, pp.98–9.

—— 1971, *The Bell Jar*, Harper & Row, New York. First published in 1962.

—— 1962, *The Poet Speaks*, Argo Record Co., No. RG455 Lm.

Sexton, A 1963, 'Sylvia's Death', available online at http://www.sylviaplath.de/plath/sexton.html#SD

Shakespeare, W 1978, *The Tempest*, Oxford University Press, London.

Stevenson, A 1989, *Bitter Fame: A Life of Sylvia Plath*, Houghton Mifflin, Boston.